INDOOR PLANTS

INDOOR PLANTS

Lovell Benjamin

Octopus Books

Contents

First published 1973 by Octopus Books Limited
59 Grosvenor Street, London W1

© 1973 Octopus Books Limited

ISBN 0 7064 0264 2

Distributed in Australia by
Rigby Limited
30 North Terrace, Kent Town
Adelaide, South Australia 5067

Produced by Mandarin Publishers Limited
14 Westlands Road, Quarry Bay, Hong Kong
and printed in Hong Kong

Introduction

There is something inherent in most human beings that makes them want to grow something. It might be a throwback to earlier times when every man had a small piece of ground on which he could raise food. In the past, cottagers who had well-filled flower gardens, dripping with colour during the summer, continued their growing efforts indoors during the winter, filling their small, latticed windows with geraniums, fuchsias, begonias and a whole host of other plants growing in pots.

This tradition lives today, although perhaps the plants that people now grow indoors are rather more sophisticated than those found in the past in cottage windows and the front parlours of town houses. Most of them are included in what has come to be known as 'house plants' together with a range of other flowering plants. It needs little more than a quiet stroll on any day in the year to confirm the popularity of indoor gardening. It is difficult to pass a house or flat, irrespective of the social standing of the occupants, that is not displaying a number of house-plants on its window-sills. Sometimes there are so many that it is difficult to believe that there is any space left. In many cases the plants must be preventing sunshine from penetrating deep into the room. So dense are they in some windows that one cannot help wondering whether the rooms inside are equally cluttered up with these beautiful plants. This very thought prompts a warning. If there are too many present, house plants lose one of their most valuable qualities—that of giving accent to decor. So unless you just want to be an enthusiastic plant grower and nothing else, choose your house plants with discretion and do not overdo it. It might amaze some that there are authorities who claim that there are over 50 million house plants gracing the homes of the British people, and a total many times greater in the United States, Australasia and European countries. This indeed is a lot and it is not surprising that you cannot go anywhere without encountering some of them.

Apart from the suggestion that there are so many because everybody keenly desires to grow something, there might be other reasons why they are so popular in modern times. Probably economics has played an important part in their rise to popularity. Many women, whether they are single or married, go out to work. In most cases, while to a comparative few this is their counter to boredom, economics is the driving force. A lot of them, however, like to have floral decorations in their home and flowers at any time are expensive, the cost becoming almost prohibitive at certain seasons. Not only are they costly to buy but anybody who loves flowers in the house is faced with a continual expense. What is more, over their short period of beautiful display they usually need almost daily attention—changing the water, shortening the stems, putting into the cool at night, wrapping in paper when

their heads droop because of weak necks and so on. Most working wives, who have to cope as well with their household duties, really have not the time for this cosseting, after a hard day's work.

The answer lies with the indoor plant. Although house plants are perhaps initially expensive, with care they can last for a number of years and prove to be bargains in the long run. Moreover many of them produce offspring without any difficulty that happily create a line of succession for the future. Even a flowering pot plant such as an Indian azalea or a cyclamen will remain in bloom and give pleasure for two or three months, outstripping a whole procession of bunches of cut flowers, and still be prepared to reappear in a blaze of colour in future years. Moreover, as the easy-to-grow indoor plants will usually flourish with no more than weekly attention, they are not much trouble. If some cacti are chosen, they can be almost neglected and still perform admirably provided they are given adequate light.

Although the advent of house plants has been acclaimed as something which happened in the twentieth century, as with so many other things there is nothing new in them. There is little doubt that plants growing in tubs and pots were brought in to decorate the house during the earlier civilisations of Rome, Egypt and India.

Although they have become universally popular during the past thirty years, many of them are the hot-house plants that were brought during the eighteenth and nineteenth century from distant climes to grace the drawing rooms and winter gardens of the rich. What is new about them is that they are now enjoyed by millions living under widely differing circumstances.

The house plant that was among the earliest to be found in all walks of life is the aspidistra, which is nowadays so prized for its magnificent, shiny, dark green leaves by flower arrangers. Introduced from China in the early nineteenth century, it was first cosseted and grown in the heated conservatory, but eventually showed itself to be the tough customer that was able to withstand the pollution of industrial towns and extremes of temperature.

The history of the many beautiful, exotic indoor plants that give so much pleasure at the present time is often most intriguing, but here we must limit our discussions into the past to the last twenty-five years. During that time there has been a great revival of interest in the United Kingdom, spread from Europe and the United States where indoor plants had long been fashionable. The cult was most advanced in Scandinavia and Holland.

Modern architecture and building techniques have had a very marked influence on this development. For success, most house plants must have adequate light and modern designed houses and commercial premises exploit this characteristic to the utmost. In many present-day houses, windows are replacing solid walls, giving in some cases a glass wall on two sides of the room, letting in every bit of sunlight and brightness, and providing the maximum illumination on dull days.

While there are climates in the world where the temperature is high enough for exotic plants to be indifferent to whether they are outdoors or in the house, walls of glass have great drawbacks in the United Kingdom, the more temperate zones of the United States and Australasia, Scandinavia, Holland and others, where in some cases there might be long spells of

bright sunshine but where temperatures fall in winter to quite uncomfortable levels. Under these circumstances an excessive amount of glass does much to increase the discomfort of the occupiers, both human and plant.

Fortunately modern builders have provided factors that offset these disadvantages. The first of these is central heating, which enables a house to be maintained comfortably warm throughout at a steady temperature. The second is the modern technique of heat insulation, which includes the use of thermal blocks in house construction, double glazing, which prevents, by means of a layer of air, heat losses and also eliminates draught, and the lining of roofs with non-conducting material.

These assets of modern living, therefore, give light, warmth and reduce fluctuations of temperature and so provide the conditions which most indoor plants need for their well-being, without the need to build special structures. These facilities were more common at an earlier date in the United States and Scandinavia than in Britain.

The intention of this book is to deal with a range of indoor plants and includes, therefore, a number of different groups that are popularly grown indoors. As there are several different categories of these and there are some people who are not completely aware of the differences, it is thought that at this stage it might be as well to become somewhat prosaic and give briefly a few definitions.

House plants are characterised by usually giving a permanent display of foliage, with some producing exquisite flowers as well, and in addition, in some cases, an exquisite loveliness with their architectural or unusual form. At no time are house plants out of beauty.

It may be a matter of commercial expediency, but we seem to have been led to think that house plants are a special category, which embraces such glorious specimens as the exotic bromeliads, the picturesque *Aphelandra,* the giant, stately *Monsteria deliciosa* and a number of other fascinating creations, that are so magnificently displayed in plant shops. There is, however, nothing in this definition that excludes the many beautiful, easily grown cacti, ferns and palms that are obtainable.

Perhaps equally as popular as house plants are flowering pot plants. Some of these are different from house plants in having, like many other plants, a period of resting after they have flowered, during which they will lose their leaves if they are deciduous and in most cases will look so miserable that they have to be hastily put out of sight. This shortcoming nevertheless is usually compensated for by their comparatively long period of flowering and their great beauty that can outshine that of the flowering house plants.

This book sets out to tell the story of indoor plants in pictures. In the hope that it will encourage novices to begin to grow them and the more experienced to meet the challenge that more difficult plants present, it is divided into chapters dealing with the different types of plants, and each chapter is further divided into 'easy-to-grow plants' and 'harder-to-grow plants'.

The foliage plants are divided according to whether they are small or large in size, whether they have outstanding beautiful foliage or any other characteristics. The flowering plants, both house and pot, are put into categories according to the season at which they flower so that it is possible to maintain a display of colour throughout the year. Bulbs are scheduled by whether they are annual or permanent.

Orchids, which are not usually dealt with in books of this type, are discussed in this one because some species do not need elaborate hothouses and can be easily grown in the house. It is hoped that this section will encourage readers to begin to cultivate the simpler types and the experienced among them to turn their hand to the harder-to-grow species and thus create for themselves a new and absorbing hobby.

Bonsai is all too briefly dealt with in this book but it is hoped that house plant enthusiasts will seek more knowledge on this fascinating Japanese art as a result of its mention.

In conclusion, the final sections deal with the use of indoor plants in decor, both from a utilitarian and aesthetic aspect A series of very lovely, coloured pictures show quite conclusively how living plants can give something special to interior decoration that cannot be contributed by the most expensive fabrics and furniture.

Foliage House Plants

Climbers

Easy-to-Grow Plants

Cissus antarctica, the Kangaroo Vine, is a very easy, tough, fast-growing, self-clinging climber. It will grow up to at least 8 feet in height if given its full rein, and is therefore quite valuable to grow as a column in a fairly large space. It makes an effective plant for forming a light screen or room divider. Although better in good light, it puts up a fairly good performance in a sunless place. A very attractive variety is *C. antarctica* 'Russikivin', which has shiny, fresh green, striated leaves. Other interesting species are *Cissus discolor* with magnificently coloured foliage and the small leaved *Cissus striata*, both of which are harder to grow.

Rhoicissus rhomboidea, which is commonly known as Grape Ivy, has dark green, glossy, veined leaves, similar in shape and colour to *Cissus antarctica*, but its leaves are groups of three leaflets, whereas with the latter the leaves grow singly. It has very attractive silvery buds and tendrils. It is an excellent climbing and trailing plant and it makes very effective screens and room dividers. In addition, it can be kept bushy and compact by pinching out the growing tips of its tallest stems. It tolerates almost everything except hot, dry conditions and is among the toughest of house plants.

The heart-shaped leaves of *Philodendron scandens* give it the popular name of the 'Sweetheart Vine', but in America it is called the 'Bathroom Plant', as it likes warm, humid conditions. It is a beginner's plant. *Philodendrons* enjoy shady positions and so are satisfactory in dark corners. Like certain other plants it throws out roots from its main stems. These are known as aerial roots and if it is trained up a moss stick or totem pole, which consists of a fine mesh cylinder, filled with constantly damp moss and vermiculite, the roots will penetrate it and absorb extra nutriment.

Hedera helix 'Lutzii'. Ivies are very popular and easily grown climbing or trailing plants. Even the common ivy, *Hedera helix,* with its lovely, glossy, dark green leaves, makes a good house plant, which does not object to a moderately dark, shady, cool situation. Some of the smaller-leaved forms, such as *H. helix* 'Lutzii', are even better. Other very attractive varieties are *H. helix* 'Glacier', which has small white-edged, green leaves, *H. helix* 'Cristata', which has crinkly leaves and *H. helix* 'Sagittaefolia', which has the most unusual leaves with five lobes, the central one being very much longer than the remainder and sharply pointed.

Hedera helix 'Heisse' is another very attractive white-edged, variegated ivy. There is little difficulty in the cultivation of ivies. The first essential is that they are grown in a good moisture-retaining soil, which contains some rotted compost or peat. They do like, however, to have it a little on the acid side. They should never be allowed to dry out, although the water supply should be reduced in the winter. They do not

Cissus antartica (top)
Rhoicissus rhomboidea (bottom)

like bright light, warm conditions or constantly dry air. Spraying their leaves is very beneficial.

Hedera canariensis 'Variegata', the Canary Island Ivy, is rather less hardy and slower-growing than *helix* ivies. Ivies have many values in modern decor, such as trailing over the sides of baskets and bowls, as pinnacles in house plant arrangements and as light screens and room dividers. When used as climbers they need support. In bowls, this can be adequately provided by means of three bamboo canes either tied to form a triangle or, by driving them in, set at a slight angle, across the centre, forming a trellis by lashing to them split canes, placed horizontally about 4½ inches apart.

Hedera canariensis 'Golden Leaf' has a lightish green centre to its bright green leaves, but no gold, and red stems and stalks. A decorative ivy standard can be created by an indoor gardener who has time. A fatshedera has all its shoots cut away, except an approximately vertical one. This is staked and allowed to reach 3–4 feet high, continuously removing any side growth. The top is then removed and a horizontal cut made across the stem's cross section. Into this four 4-inch-long cuttings of ivy are inserted, bound up with raffia and tied up in a polythene bag until they take some 8–10 weeks later.

Ficus pumila is commonly called the Creeping Fig. A beginner's plant, because it is so easy to grow and a rapid grower, it is also hardy and is a good plant for a cool room. In fact in some milder districts, it survives outdoors. It dislikes direct

Philodendron scandens (bottom left)
Hedera helix 'Lutzii' (top)
Hedera helix 'Heisse' (bottom right)

sun, much preferring a shady spot. It delights in moist air and must be kept well-watered even in winter as the soil must never be allowed to dry out. Excellent as a trailer for hanging baskets and for trailing over the edges of containers, it is also a beautiful climber, by virtue of its aerial roots, which can cling to a moss stick.

Harder to Grow Plants

Scindapsus aureus, sometimes known as Devil's Ivy, is a very attractive trailing or tall-growing, climbing house plant. Both the species and its varieties have heart-shaped leaves that are variegated and resemble philodendrons. Their foliage is larger and more lush if the aerial roots, that are freely produced along their stems, are trained on a moss stick. They generally need a moist, warm, draught-free position with some shade in the summer and full light in winter. The illustration shows the variety 'Marble Queen', which is particularly beautiful with white leaves, flecked green. It requires full light but not direct sunlight, otherwise the leaves turn green.

Philodendron melanochryson, which is also known as *Philodendron andreanum* as it becomes adult, is a slender climber, which produces aerial roots. It is hard to grow, but its great beauty issues a tremendous challenge to the ambitious house plant enthusiast. The spectacular foliage is composed of 5–6 inch long, elongated, heart-shaped leaves. They are dark green with a velvet texture, with purplish pink undersides giving them the appearance of being greenish purple. To thrive, it is necessary to keep it in a warm, humid, atmosphere of about 18°C. (65°F.).

Opposite page
Hedera canariensis 'Variegata' (top left)
Hedera canariensis 'Golden Leaf' (top right)
Ficus pumila (bottom)

This page
Philodendron melanochryson (top)
Scindapsus aureus (bottom)

Trailers

Easy-to-Grow Plants

Known variously by the names—Wandering Jew, Travelling Sailor—*Tradescantia fluminensis* is a very easily grown and propagated trailer plant. It has small, pointed, striped leaves. In bright light (but not direct sunlight) pinkish tints may appear in the foliage. Its varieties, *T. fluminensis* 'Quicksilver' (top right), *T. fluminensis* 'Variegata' (bottom left) and *T. fluminensis* 'Aurea' (middle right) are all very beautiful trailers, which are most effective for wall brackets, hanging baskets, dish and bottle gardens. The remaining members of the above group are near relatives *Zebrina purpusii* (formerly known as *Tradescantia purpurea* (top left) and *Zebrina pendula* (bottom right) both with leaves beautifully coloured with purple on both sides and with an added bonus of flowers in late summer.

Chlorophytum comosum 'Variegatum' is regarded as the easiest of the foliage house plants to grow indoors and to propagate. All it needs is to be put in a bright place, out of sunlight, and to be watered well and regularly during summer, with very little in the winter. It has most lovely leaves, lengthwise striped green and white. The long arching stems bear inconspicuous whitish flowers and tiny plantlets, which, if cut off and planted, take root most easily. An effective plant for hanging baskets.

Harder-to-Grow Plants

Fittonia verschaffeltii is a very beautiful dwarf trailing plant that comes from Peru. When it is young, however, it makes quite an attractive, bushy foliage plant. It has long, pointed leaves, about 3 inches long, of dark green, somewhat bluish, with deep veins that are crimson. Its flowers, white and small, are insignificant and completely outclassed by its beautiful foliage, and are better removed as they appear. Requiring a warm room (not less than 50°F. (10°C.)) in winter and fair humidity, it is at its best in a bottle garden.

Ficus radicans 'Variegata' is a very attractive trailing plant with slender-pointed green leaves, marked with cream, that are much more pleasing than the plain green *F. radicans*. Unfortunately it is a difficult plant to grow, but it is so beautiful that it is worthwhile making a special effort to be successful and ensure that the temperature does not fall lower than 50°F. (10°C.) throughout the winter. It must always grow in a moist atmosphere. To grow it as a bushy plant pinch out the shoot tips.

Opposite page
Chlorophytum comosum 'Variegatum' (top)
Tradescantia fluminensis (bottom)

This page
Fittonia verschaffeltii (top)
Ficus radicans 'Variegata' (bottom)

Bushy

Easy-to-Grow Plants

Cyperus alternifolius is a semi-aquatic plant that originally came from the swamps of Madagascar and so, as might be expected, it likes constant humidity, which can be provided by standing it in a saucer of water. It is hardy, easy to grow and, perhaps rather oddly in view of its origin, it does not need to be placed in a heated room but does like semi-shade. The unusual growth produces rosettes of leaves at its base from which emanate flowering stems that are surmounted by crowns of leaves, like the ribs of an umbrella. Hence its popular name, the Umbrella Plant.

Helxine soleirolii, which rejoices in the various nicknames, Mind Your Own Business, Baby's Tears, and Irish or Japanese Moss, is a charming dwarf plant that natively creeps over the ground in Corsica. Fantastically easy to grow, it is a water-lover and one of the few indoor plants that can flourish when its pot is kept standing in a saucer of water. The foliage must not, however, be wetted in winter, because it is liable to rot. It is a most valuable house plant because it can carpet the soil beneath either a single plant or a group.

Aspidistra lurida, the Cast Iron Plant, Parlour Palm, was a favourite during the nineteenth century and the earlier decades of the twentieth, but although much cherished by flower arrangers, particularly in its variegated form, it is something of a rarity nowadays, because, being a slow grower, it is costly to raise. Tough, as its first popular name suggests, it tolerates gas fumes, shade, dust, dry air and soil, but dislikes bright sunshine. What it likes ideally is to be given a reasonable supply of moisture, medium humidity and fair warmth. It loves a day out in warm, summer rain and regular washing with tepid water.

Gynura Velvet Purple Plant is a plant which is a multi-purpose one, making both an excellent trailer or a bushy house plant. It is converted into the latter by pinching out the points of the shoots. It can also be trained up small canes and then becomes an attractive climber, reaching a height of 18 inches. On the other hand, it is beautiful in a hanging basket, if it is allowed to grow loosely over the edge. It appreciates central heating, good lighting and in the summer plenty of water. *Gynura sarmentosa* produces evil-smelling orange flowers that must be picked off.

Sansevieria trifasciata 'Laurentii' is, perhaps rather un-kindly, commonly called Mother-in-law's Tongue; the alter-native is Snake Plant. This is a beautiful house plant with gorgeously coloured leaves, reaching 24 inches or more in length. They are stiff, thick and fleshy and, rather intriguingly, slightly twisted. It is a valuable plant, which is especially useful in dish gardens, where it not only gives great character, but also height. Easy to grow, providing it is not given too much water—weekly in summer and monthly in winter—it has the unusual quality of being able to stand direct sunshine.

Saxifraga sarmentosa, also known botanically as *S. stoloni-fera.* This is an easy-to-grow plant that does best in a cool room and when kept moist. It likes to be in a light position, but abhors sunshine, and flourishes better when planted in a small pot. It is a pretty, small plant with very lovely strawberry-like, dark green leaves with whitish cream veins. As seen on page 16, interesting colour is added by the purplish hue

under its leaves. The hair-like runners, which it sends out, develop plantlets at their tips and these may easily be rooted. Popular names are Mother of Thousands and Loving Sailor.

Setcreasea purpurea is a lovely house plant, which has more recently been introduced from Mexico. It is a quick-grower and an easy plant to cultivate. The lance-shaped leaves are 6 inches long and about 1¼ inches wide, with long, white hairs on their surfaces, which give a fascinating haziness to their purplish green and violet colour. Placed in a good light these tints are intensified and it does not object to sunshine. It will survive during the winter in an unheated room. It makes an attractive member of an arrangement, where it tends to trail over the rim of the container.

The Norfolk Island Pine, *Auricaria excelsa,* grown as a house plant is really a bonsai, because when growing naturally it reaches 100 to 150 feet. A very hardy house plant, it is very easy to grow and if kept in a cool room and out of draughts, it will grow slowly for a long time with little that can go wrong. Providing the soil is kept moist it needs little attention. Given a warmer atmosphere, it will become quite sizable and can be used quite attractively in larger spaces. It is valuable as a Christmas tree that serves from year to year.

Opposite page
Cyperus alternifolius (top)
Helxine soleirolii (centre)
Aspidistra lurida (bottom)

This page
Sansevieria trifasciata 'Laurentii' (top)
Gynura aurantiaca (bottom)

Fatsia japonica, which is known as the Fig Leaf Palm and commonly, but erroneously, as the Castor Oil Plant. One of the hardiest of foliage house plants, it will flourish in temperate climates, in shady spots out of doors. As an indoor plant, it grows easily and can become quite large and so is useful in larger spaces. It does not require warmth during winter nor does it need bright light but it should be copiously watered during summer. The large shiny leaves should be sponged occasionally and the plant will appreciate a day out in the summer rain. A variegated form is obtainable.

Fatshedera lizei, which is also called Fat-headed Lizzie or the Ivy Tree, is botanically unusual as it is a cross between two genera, *Fatsia* and *Hedera* (Ivy). It has a more climbing habit than *Fatsia*, with leaves that have its texture and colour, but tending towards the ivy in shape. As might be expected it has the qualities of both. It grows easily in a cold or average room, needing no heat in winter. Keep it out of direct sunlight and well-watered, but not excessively, except in winter when it should be kept on the dry side. The picture shows *Fatshedera lizei* 'Variegata', a flower arranger's favourite.

Saxifraga sarmentosa (top)
Setcreasea purpurea (bottom)
Auricaria excelsa (opposite)

There is nothing more truly descriptive of *Ficus elastica* 'Decora', the India-rubber Plant, than the word 'Decora', meaning handsome. It is indeed a good looking plant that will eventually grow 8 feet or more high and is suitable for large areas. The dark green, shiny leaves, which are 9–12 inches long and 5–7 inches wide, emerge from a colourful red sheath. It withstands, in the absence of draughts, high and low temperatures, providing it is kept moist in summer and fairly dry in winter. It does not like direct sunlight. *Ficus elastica* 'Robusta' is regarded by some as better and more robust.

Ficus benjamina 'the Weeping Fig or Willow Fig' is more difficult to cultivate than other species of *Ficus,* but following the rules, it is not so hard a task. The temperature of the room in which it is kept should not fall below 50°F. (10°C.).

Fatsia japonica (top left)
Fatshedera lizei (top right)
Ficus elastica 'Decora' (bottom left)
Ficus benjamina (bottom right)

It must always be kept moist in summer, allowing it to dry out almost between waterings but should be kept out of direct sunlight. Some of its leaves are lost naturally during the winter, so this should not cause alarm. Although it is valuable in a pot or group, it will grow to a tall, handsome, weeping tree.

Ficus pandurata or *F. lyrata* is more commonly known as the Fiddle-leaved Fig or Fiddleleaf, which picturesque names it owes to the shape of its leaves. It is a handsome plant, which has very lovely, large, shiny, medium green leaves, strikingly marked with cream-coloured veins. Although a little more difficult to grow, it needs similar treatment to *F. elastica* 'Decora'. Under perfect conditions, *F. pandurata* will eventually reach tree-like dimensions. A very beautiful plant for offices and other more spacious premises which fortunately can be controlled by severe pruning.

The Australian Wattle or Silk Oak, *Grevillea robusta,* is wrongfully regarded by some people as a fern, because of its very pleasing, silvery, finely divided foliage. It is, however, less trouble to grow in an ordinary living room than most ferns, so it has become a much appreciated substitute. Very easy to grow and most adaptable, requiring neither warmth in the winter nor a humid atmosphere, it does not, however, like cold draughts. Eventually outstripping any house room for size, it is, however, marvellous decoration for an office, showroom or hotel foyer. It grows easily from seed.

Monstera pertusa is a giant foliage plant and, when allowed to grow freely under favourable conditions, it becomes one of the largest of the indoor plants. As a result, it is very popular for offices, shops, public buildings and other roomy places. Fortunately it is most effective in a container, because due to the root restriction, it grows pretty slowly. The height can be

Ficus pandurata (top)
Grevillea robusta (bottom)

controlled by cutting out its top periodically. Perhaps its most grand feature is its enormous, dark green, slashed and perforated leaves, which make a dramatic contrast with the very glossy and delicate green, new leaves as they appear.

Monstera deliciosa has different popular names, including Gruyère Cheese Plant, Swiss Cheese Plant, Mexican Breadfruit, Ceriman and Fruit Salad Plant, which refer to the curious leaf form or its fruit. The edible part is the pulp around the spalix as seen developing in this illustration, and has an elusive flavour. Easy to grow, *Monstera* tends to like warmth, but adapts itself to cool, good humidity, plenty of water, with pretty dry intervals, and feeding during the summer. It produces abundant aerial roots, that may be tied together and should be inserted in the soil.

Philodendron bipinnatifidum is a most imposing member of the large, impressive genus, *Philodendron*, which includes among its members both climbing and bushy plants. There are also a number of very beautiful foliage plants to be found in this plant group, some of which eventually become very big and make excellent shrubs in tubs, standing on the floor in large areas. Among the more common of these is *Philodendron bipinnatifidum* which is so frequently seen in florists. It is an easy-to-grow, tall, graceful plant with leaves that are 2½ feet long and 1½ feet wide and have a refreshing bright colour.

Schlefflera actinophylla, which is shown in the picture below, is an example of how confusing popular names of house plants can be, because this, in common with *Cyperus alternifolius*, is called the Umbrella Tree, despite the vast difference that exists between them. It is one of the most luxuriant of green-leaved house plants. Its glossy, green, long, pointed leaves grow in groups of three or five at the top of individual leaf stems, like the ribs of an umbrella. Doing well under almost any conditions, it grows fairly quickly and will eventually become very large, making an excellent office plant.

Philodendron bipinnatifidum (top)
Monstera pertusa (bottom left)
Schlefflera actinophylla (bottom right)
Monstera deliciosa (opposite)

Plants with Especially Beautiful Foliage

Begonia rex. The begonias belong to a large genus of widely varying plants. Some are grown for their decorative foliage, such as *Begonia rex,* whose leaves are as colourful as flowers, while in others their outstanding beauty lies in their blooms. *Begonia rex,* although it is a delicate plant, is not found too difficult by many indoor gardeners. It should be grown in semi-shade, out of reach of gas fumes and kept in an outer container filled with moist peat. Water well during the summer, less in winter, keeping water off its leaves. Winter temperature should be above 50°–55°F. (10°–13°C.).

The beauty of *Begonia masoniana* lies in its remarkably patterned leaves rather than gorgeously coloured foliage. The noticeably bright green leaves, with pointed tips, have superimposed a distinctive, curious purplish-black cross reminiscent of the German award. So close is the resemblance that this species has become known as the Iron Cross begonia. It is slower growing than *Begonia rex,* but its cultivation is much the same. Contributing to its beauty, it has fleshy, red-pink stems, which contrast magnificently with the brilliant green foliage. It is one of the finest of the begonias.

Cordyline terminalis with its tapering leaves, which are up to 12 inches in length and 4 inches wide, coloured brilliant green and red, intensified in bright light, is one of the most beautiful foliage house plants. It rarely exceeds 2 feet in height.

Begonia rex (top left)
Begonia masoniana (bottom left)
Cordyline terminalis (top right)
Cordyline terminalis 'Firebrand' (bottom right)
Pileas (opposite)

The soil should be rich and contain a good amount of peat or leaf-mould. It should be kept at 55°–61°F. (13°–16°C.) during summer, when it should be well watered, reducing considerably in the winter. Cordylines are sometimes confused with the dracaenas, which they resemble. Popular names are the Flaming Dragon Tree or, even more spectacularly, the Scarlet Aspidistra.

Cordyline terminalis 'Firebrand' is a charming variety. The very lovely multicoloured leaves of pink, green, cream, red and other colours puts it high up in the scale of merit for foliage beauty.

The pileas below form an interesting group. Bushy plants, they are quick-growing and easy-to-grow and are distinguished by their very fascinating foliage markings. These attractive plants are valuable to the indoor gardener, because of their versatility; they are equally at home as the low components of a dish garden as they are when included in a bottle garden. The plants shown in the illustration are: the Aluminium or Friendship Plant. *Pilea cadierei* (top)—there is also a very lovely dwarf version of this species—*P. cadierei* 'Nana', *P. spruceana* 'Bronze' (bottom right) and *P. cadierei* 'Moon Valley'.

Pilea cadierei 'Moon Glow' is another very lovely foliage plant. Like other pileas, it is easy to grow. In common with the others, it likes to be kept reasonably warm and its soil never allowed to become dry. It does not mind whether it is put in bright light or semi-shade and is thus valuable for a moderately dark room. All pileas dislike draughts and gas fumes. If its stems are periodically pinched off at their ends, bushiness is maintained. Another species, *Pilea muscosa*, the Artillery Plant, with its moss-like leaves, makes a very beautiful plant for hanging baskets.

Rhoeo discolor is a beautiful, large foliage house plant. It is an interesting example of how popular plant names are derived. Because it has pretty, blue or white, but insignificant flowers, contained in purple boat- or cradle-shaped bracts at the base of its leaves, it has become popularly known as the Boat Lily or Moses in the Rushes. Its real beauty lies in its dark green, long leaves, that are rose-purple underneath. It likes plenty of water, some shade and its leaves sprayed in summer, and a minimum winter temperature of 50°F. (10°C.). It makes a good tub plant.

Pilea cadierei 'Moon Glow' (top)
Rhoeo discolor (bottom)

Bromeliads

The bromeliad, *Cryptanthus zonatus*, 'Chameleon or Earth Star', has the fascinating ability to change its colour according to whether it is placed in the sun or not, as is strikingly shown in the two illustrations. It is a very popular house plant that gives much glamour to dish-gardens and bottle gardens. Perhaps one of the most attractive ways of displaying *Cryptanthus* is to allow them to grow on an old log or piece of bark, as they do in nature rather than in a pot. To do this, the plant should be removed from its container, its roots wrapped in a ball of fresh sphagnum moss. The combination should then be tied to the wood. The plant is watered either by spraying the moss covering or by plunging the plant plus its anchorage into a bucket of luke-warm water. *Cryptanthus zonatus* needs fair moisture during the summer season, without over-watering. Cool winter temperatures do no harm, but little watering is necessary.

Another member of the pineapple family is the variegated pineapple, *Ananas comosum* 'Variegatus'. This is also a very beautiful house plant, with long serrated pointed leaves, with lengthwise stripes, green in the centre flanked by yellow, tinged red towards the margins.

Cryptanthus zonatus (top and bottom)

Neoregelia carolinae 'Tricolor' is an easy bromeliad to grow. Its saw-toothed leaves, 12–15 inches long and 1–1½ inches wide, are green with an inner, lengthwise-running stripe of cream, becoming pink at their bases, where they form a cup-shaped depression, pink in colour. Just before the inconspicuous flowers appear, it becomes vivid scarlet. It prefers to be placed in the shade or semi-shade, but it does not mind a dry atmosphere. In summer, keep the cup full of tepid water. When the flowers fade they become evil-smelling and should be removed with tweezers and the cup washed out.

Nidularium fulgens, often known as the Bird's Nest Bromeliad, is an epiphytic bromeliad, which means that when it grows naturally it attaches itself to another plant. It is a native of Southern Brazil. The main, long, green leaves are about 12 inches long and 2 inches wide. In the centre, as seen in the illustration, there are 6 to 10 short, scarlet leaves. After the rather insignificant flowers die, the centre of the rosette must be kept filled with water. An easy plant to grow in a pot, it does well without much light and should preferably be kept at a moderate, even temperature.

Neoregelia carolinae 'Tricolor' (top)
Nidularium fulgens (bottom)

Harder-to-Grow Plants

Aglaonema commutatum is also known as the Chinese Evergreen, a name which is something of an anomaly. This rather beautiful foliage plant does not, in fact, come from China, but from the Philippines. This very compact and most attractive plant, with its dark green, glossy, lanceolate leaves, that are 9 inches long and have chevron-shaped markings of white, is worth trying to grow. It should be kept in the shade at 60°–70°F. (15°–21°C.), well moist during the summer, but little watered in winter and away from gas fumes. In hot weather, it appreciates regular spraying with clean water. While growing it should be fed with liquid manure.

Peperomia caperata is the best known of a very delightful group of house plants, which are excellent for bottle gardens as well as dishes. Its attractiveness lies in its unusual, dark green and crinkled leaves, that are carried on colourful pink stems. Although having little floral beauty, it produces large numbers of curious cream-coloured flowers, close to their brown, erect stems, which curve over at the tip to form what look like miniature shepherd's crooks. There are also a number of trailing peperomias which are particularly lovely when falling over the rim of a container. Variegated *P. scandens* is a pleasing example.

Peperomia caperata (top)
Aglaonema commutatum (bottom)

(top) *Peperomia magnoliaefolia*
'Variegata' (top right) and
Peperomia caperata 'Tricolor' (left)
Peperomia hederaefolia (bottom)

A very similar, but larger relative of *Peperomia caperata*, is *Peperomia hederaefolia*. A compact plant, at 6 inches high, its leaves are very much less corrugated than those of *P. caperata* and have a metallic, greyish green colour. The somewhat similar white or yellowish flowers are borne on narrow spikes, but while they are not beautiful, they contrast excellently with its massed foliage. It is rather more tender than *P. caperata*. All the peperomias, many of which have attractively patterned foliage, belong to the Pepper family, which contains a large number of species, and comes mostly from tropical America.

The illustration above shows two very charming and useful peperomias—top, right, *Peperomia magnoliaefolia* 'Variegata' and bottom, left, *P. caperata* 'Tricolor'. The former is also known as *Peperomia obtusifolia* 'Variegata'. All peperomias require a warm place, where there is good humidity, and like to be in shade. They have small roots and need to be planted in small pots, in which the drainage is good. They need to be frequently watered in summer, but never over-watered and to be kept drier during the winter months. Avoid splashing their leaves and crown, because this might lead to rotting.

Plants with Especially Beautiful Foliage

Caladium candidum, perhaps the most spectacular of foliage house plants, is extremely hard to grow, but it is so beautiful that it is worth being persistent with it so that it can be used to adorn hanging baskets or table decorations. To be successful, it should be wintered in a greenhouse maintained at 60°F. (15·5°C.), though some people find it easier to buy new plants each year. It needs plenty of light, but not hot sunshine. The white-leaved plant shown in the illustration is *C. candidum*; the one with the carmine-coloured centre is 'Frieda Hemple' and the third is 'Pink Beauty'.

Calathea mackoyana, which is popularly known as the Peacock Plant is a strikingly marked foliage plant. It is a member of a large family that is indigenous to South America. This is the best known of the calatheas; it resembles a *Maranta*, and is sometimes sold under that name. It is difficult to grow indoors. So much so that it is probably better to regard it as an expendable plant and to replace it every year or so. Because of its great demand for humidity and warmth, it is most satisfactory when it is grown in a bottle garden.

Another calathea, *Calathea insignis*, is shown overleaf. It is less colourful than *C. mackoyana*, but is nevertheless very attractive and catches the eye in any arrangement. Like all of them, it is not very easy to grow, but if it is decided to meet the challenge, here is what must be done. Plant it in a rich, open soil ($\frac{1}{2}$ peat or leaf-mould and $\frac{1}{2}$ light loam). Keep it in the shade, out of draughts, at a temperature of not less than 60°F. (15·5°C.). Water well during summer, plunge in moist peat and spray its leaves. Give little water in the winter.

Caladium candidum (top)
Calathea mackoyana (bottom)

Codiaeum variegatum pictum is also known as the South Sea Laurel, though another popular name of this plant, and its numerous lovely varieties, is Croton and they are mostly sold under that name. They are gaudy, tropical shrubs with tough, evergreen leaves. These are various in shape and are patterned in a range of colours—yellow, scarlet, green, white and pink. *C. variegatum pictum* is a difficult plant to grow, but is worthwhile persisting with, because of the glamour of its wonderful multi-coloured foliage. A particularly beautiful, rather slower-growing croton, is *Codiaeum* 'Van Ostensee', which has thin, narrow, grass-like, coloured leaves.

A rather unusual plant, *Codiaeum* 'Madame Mayne' is illustrated opposite. Like the other codiaeums, it is by no means an easy plant to grow. In common with other members of the family, the temperature of the surrounding air must never fall below 55°F. (13°C.) and there should be no great fluctuations. No matter what happens, draughts must be excluded and the plants must not stand in sunshine. Perhaps most important of all, they must be kept in a moist atmosphere by syringing the leaves and plunging in peat. Using tepid water when watering is advantageous.

Another variety is *Codiaeum* 'Emperor Alexander II'. Codiaeums in common with *Cordyline, Dieffenbachia, Ficus* and others, eventually lose their lower leaves. As this is an inevitable process a good solution, to avoid having increasingly leggy plants, is to air-layer them. This consists of cutting a narrow ring in the bark, 12 inches below the tip, and after moistening it, rooting compound is applied. A good handful of moist sphagnum moss is tied round it with raffia, and

Codiaeum variegatum pictum (top)
Calathea insignis (bottom)
(opposite) *Codiaeum* 'Madame Mayne' (top)
Codiaeum 'Emperor Alexander II' (bottom)

covered with polythene, affixed with sticky tape. When roots appear, the stem is cut just below the bundle, the wrapping removed, and the new plant is potted. The remaining stem is reduced then to soil level and with watering and feeding new shoots will appear.

The plant in the illustration left is 'Red Edge', a very charming variety of *Dracaena*. Most of the dracaenas that are grown as house plants nowadays are natives of Tropical Africa, which means that, while they grow under average room conditions, to be at their best they need to be kept in a very warm place, where the atmosphere is moist. These are the conditions to which they have been accustomed in their natural surroundings. There is indeed much that can be learnt about house plants, if an enthusiast studies the climate of the places where they are indigenous.

Another worthy species is *Dracaena bausei*, which has silver-centred leaves with margins of green, with silver-coloured stems. To be successful with dracaenas, give them a warm spot (with a few exceptions, never lower than 55°F. (13°C.) in the winter) and humidity. Water freely in the summer, but far less in winter. Syringe and feed regularly, while growing. They like both light and semi-shade.

Dracaena sanderiana (sanderi) is one of the most popular of the dracaenas, and is known as the Variegated Dragon Tree. As will be seen in the picture, it has lance-shaped leaves, that are 3–4 inches long and 1 inch across. They are brilliant green

in the centre, with some striating of a lighter tone, with a white margin. More delicate than some species it requires a moist air at a temperature of 65°–70°F. (18°–21°C.). It is also rather smaller than some and so is most effective when planted in groups of three in a 5 inch pot or in a bottle garden.

Fittonia argyroneura, the Snake Skin Plant, is a low-growing plant, with roundish leaves, coloured medium green with deep silver veins, which combine together to give the plant an attractive bluish green appearance. It is a difficult house plant to grow outside a bottle garden, because it has a constant need of humidity and warmth, but it cannot stand great heat. It requires a minimum temperature of 13°C. (55°F.). While it should not be allowed to get too dry overwatering is also detrimental and a careful balance must be maintained. When outside a bottle keep the plant away from draughts and plunge its pot into damp peat.

Dracaena 'Red Edge' (opposite top)
Dracaena sanderiana (opposite bottom)
Fittonia argyroneura (below)

Maranta leuconeura 'Kerchoveana' is a remarkable plant, because at sunset its leaves lift upward and clasp together like hands in prayer, and then unfold again in the morning. For this reason, it is popularly known as the Prayer Plant. But this is not all; it has a wealth of common names. Because of the smudged, brownish black markings on its leaves, it has become called Rabbit's Tracks. It is sometimes called the Arrowroot Plant, but this is erroneous, because it is *Maranta arundinacea*, from which this starchy food is obtained. Lastly, for less obvious reasons, it is termed 'Husband and Wife Plant'.

Maranta leuconeura 'Erythrophylla', with its fantastically coloured leaves and reddish veins, perhaps strangely, does not seem to have a popular name, although justifiably it has been called 'the Fishbone Plant'; and because of the leaf colourings it is sometimes sold as *Maranta tricolor*. Needing warmth and a moist atmosphere, marantas may be difficult to grow outside a bottle garden, for which they make most attractive occupants. If attempted outside a bottle, they should be kept out of draughts and at a minimum temperature of 13°C. (55°F.), in a shady spot and with the pot surrounded with damp peat. They appreciate feeding while growing.

Plants with Especially Beautiful Foliage

Aralia elegantissima (Dizygotheca elegantissima) is a dainty-leaved plant with narrow, delicately fingered, serrated leaves, which are not more than ½ inch across. They are splayed in an almost flat plane at the extremities of its dark green, mottled cream, stalks. With maturity they become almost black. It grows slowly and, when small, makes an excellent pinnacle in an arrangement, but a tall, mature plant is excellent for large space decoration. In winter it requires a temperature of 60°F. (15·5°C.), a moist atmosphere and good light, dislikes tem-

Maranta leuconeura 'Kerchoveana' (top)
Maranta leuconeura 'Erythrophylla' (bottom)

Dieffenbachia amoena (top)
Aralia elegantissima (bottom)
Pandanus veitchii (overleaf)

perature fluctuations, draughts and over-watering and so is not an easy plant to grow.

Dieffenbachia amoena, Dumb Cane or Mother-in-Law Plant, has one rather unfortunate characteristic in that its sap is poisonous and care should be taken to see that when cutting the cane or removing a leaf it does not enter a cut. Tall-growing, it can make an excellent office plant, particularly if the temperature is never less than 55°F. (13°C.) in winter and constant, and there is good humidity. While it must be kept well watered, avoid over-watering, and regularly syringe it during summer. Keep its pot immersed in damp peat. It tolerates dim light, but thrives in bright.

Pandanus veitchii is an attractive foliage plant with palm-like leaves, that grow to 2 feet or even longer and are green in colour, bordered with white or silver-white, with vicious spines on the margins. The plant should be placed where it cannot be easily touched. The spines are spirally arranged on the stem and for this reason it has been given its popular name of Screw Pine. Because it demands constant warmth, not below 55°F. (13°C.) in the winter, a moist atmosphere and good light, out of direct sunshine, it is regarded as a difficult plant to grow. Syringe the foliage frequently.

Flowering House Plants

Easy-to-Grow Plants

Winter-flowering
Begonia scandens 'Glaucophylla' makes a most attractive indoor climbing plant with its very charming, brick-red, pendulous flowers. The flowers stand out superbly against the background foil of greyish green, shiny, longish, pointed leaves, that hang gracefully from its delicate stems. Perhaps it is at its best when allowed to clamber up some trellis work or similar structure, when it might well make a very beautiful screen or room divider. Alternatively, this delightful plant may look lovely when grown in a hanging basket. It does not care for a hot room, but likes to grow in a moist atmosphere.

Spring-flowering
Jasminum mesnyi (primulinum) is one of those very valuable dual-purpose plants. Equally comfortable growing indoors or against a warm, sunny wall outdoors where it will reach a height of 15 feet or more. Because of this quality, it can be stood outside during the summer or be safely transplanted into a warm position in the garden, if a change of decor makes it redundant. The very lovely, bright yellow flowers show up well against its dark green, trifoliate leaves. Supported on a framework, it makes a good room divider, or pruning will keep it bushy.

Summer-flowering
Hoya carnosa is popularly known by the picturesque names of Porcelain Flower or Wax Plant. A lovely climbing plant with glossy, oval, slender-pointed, fleshy leaves and with clusters of waxen, star-shaped, pinkish-white, sweetly scented flowers with reddish pink centres from which drops of nectar are often to be found hanging. In addition, there is a variegated variety, Hoya carnosa 'Variegata', which is a rather slower grower. It has cream and white leaves. Another species, Hoya australis, has white flowers, tinged pink, with a fragrance resembling honeysuckle. They all need light, some warmth and moisture to ensure their flowering. In winter, its temperature should not be below 50°F. (10°C.).

Passiflora caerulea, the Blue Passion Flower, is a native of South Brazil. The flower filaments are violet-blue in the type and with whitish sepals, but there is in addition a pure white variety, 'Constance Elliott'. Other species and varieties of Passion Flower have red pink and purplish flowers. It is a quick-growing climbing plant, with an unusual and striking flower, that is slightly fragrant. It can make a beautiful specimen when grown in a pot and trained up two bamboo canes, set at an angle, so that the stems make a bridge across the top. To ensure flowering a sunny position is essential

Begonia scandens 'Glaucophylla' (top)
Jasminum mesnyi (bottom)

Passiflora caerulea (left)
Hoya carnosa (below)

Opposite page
Aeschynanthus speciosus (top)
Columnea (bottom left)
Stephanotis floribunda (bottom right)

Harder-to-Grow Plants

Winter-flowering
Columnea. Although it is possible to tie some species of *Columnea* to supports, the plants are far better as trailers than climbers and amongst the most beautiful. The flowers are usually reddish orange, and appear during the summer, growing on either side of long pendulous stems. In their native habitats, the columneas, of which there are many, grow from the branches of trees, which makes them a natural for hanging baskets. They are very demanding, requiring constant warmth and humidity, with liberal watering during the growing season. They like good light without direct sunlight.

Summer-flowering
Aeschynanthus speciosus is another house plant that can either be used as a climber by supporting it, with short pea sticks or with bamboo canes, or as a trailer growing either in a pot or hanging basket. Its clusters of six to twenty rich orange, turning yellow towards the base, tubular-shaped, scented flowers, give a wonderful display in the house during the summer. It should not be allowed to flower during its first summer. It needs much water during the summer, with little during the winter. It should be repotted every year, using a mixture of sifted leaf-mould and sphagnum moss.

Stephanotis floribunda is an extremely beautiful flower as shown in the illustration. With the similarity of its blooms to *Jasminum polyanthum*, it is understandable that it is known as the Madagascar Jasmine, as it is a native of this Indian Ocean island. Its waxen, white flowers have a rich scent, which can be overpowering in a small room. They grow in clusters or bunches along the length of its stems, which need supporting. It should be kept fairly warm, and never below 55°F. (13°C.) during winter, with its pot surrounded by damp peat and occasionally sprayed to maintain the humidity.

Bushy and Upright Plants

Easy-to-Grow Plants

Spring-flowering
Clivia miniata is popularly known as the Kafir Lily. Reputedly as tough and long-lasting as the aspidistra, it has very pleasing, orange or red, funnel-shaped flowers amid its fleshy, strap-like, green leaves. Needing lots of light, but no direct sunlight, a window-sill facing north is an excellent position for it. It likes plenty of water and feeding during the summer and to be kept relatively dry in winter. Washing and syringing the leaves during warm weather is very much appreciated.

Summer-flowering
Beloperone guttata. Because of the brownish rose-coloured bracts, which resemble shrimps, the popular name of this unusual, beautiful, exotic plant is the Shrimp Plant. The soft, shining green leaves are an added attraction. Perhaps, because of the ease with which it grows and its unusualness, it has become a popular house plant. It loves a sunny window and should be given plenty of water during spring and summer, but be kept rather dry and cool during winter. Occasional spraying during hot weather is beneficial. Pruning in spring encourages new growth and pinching out the tops keeps it bushy.

Beloperone guttata (top)
Clivia miniata (bottom)

Impatiens petersiana (top)
Begonia semperflorens (bottom)

Flowering all the Year Round

Begonia semperflorens. This lovely begonia species is the most widely grown and gives considerable pleasure in the home for most of the year. It is a sun-lover and a gas fume-hater. Water freely throughout the summer without wetting the leaves, but give only little in winter, when the temperature should be maintained at 50°–55°F. (10°–13°C.). There is a range of white, pink, red and deep crimson among the flower colours as well as green and brownish leaved varieties. Interesting cultivars are 'Aloha', with its salmon-orange flowers and 'Curly Locks', whose pink blooms are crested yellow and leaves are dark copper.

Impatiens. The several nicknames—Busy Lizzie, Patient Lucy and the Patience Plant—are no doubt an indication of the long-established popularity of various species of this plant, that always seems to be in flower. Dwarf varieties are available. The picture shows a plant with the carmine-red flowers typical of *I. petersiana,* a plant which some authorities consider a variety of *I. holstii. I. holstii* has bright scarlet flowers and *I. sultanii* various colours: the hybrids between these two perennial species having orange, red, pink, white, carmine and violet flowers. *I. balsamina* is an annual and has varieties with white, pink, purple and red shades of flower and in single or double form. Most do well with plenty of moisture and survive full sun during the summer. Warmth and sufficient moisture to prevent flagging are needed in the colder months.

Harder-to-grow Plants

Winter- and Early Spring-Flowering
Saintpaulia ionantha, which is known as the African Violet, is the favourite among the house plants. Saintpaulias are very difficult to maintain successfully, especially in houses without central heating, because their demands are so exacting and thousands of those bought or received as gifts annually come to grief. They are most effective, for example, when potted up singly, to be displayed individually, or in groups, on side-tables, or as a centre piece to a dining-room table; or used as a colourful foil to taller neighbours in an arrangement; or placed on a tiered stand to form a colourful feature.

The picture below shows a beautiful, soft, pink variety of *Saintpaulia.* In addition to violet and pink, there are white cultivars. The essential ingredients of successful cultivation are warmth, light and humidity. Saintpaulias require a moderate, steady heat, that maintains a temperature never below 60°F. (15·5°C.) by day and 50°F. (10°C.) by night. This is fairly easy in a centrally-heated room. They must have good light, but must not be exposed to direct sunlight. It has been established that saintpaulias should have 14 hours light each 24 hours, which in winter must be partly natural and partly artificial.

Saintpaulia ionantha 'Englert's Diana' is a lovely named variety. To grow successfully, African Violets must have a moist atmosphere, which can be quite effectively created by surrounding the pot with moist peat contained in a second or by standing it on a wet pebble tray (see page 99). In addition, they benefit by being given a steam bath occasionally. This is

made by placing a wooden block in a basin and pouring in boiling water nearly up to its top. The saintpaulia is stood on

Saintpaulia ionantha (top)
Saintpaulia ionantha pink variety (bottom)
Saintpaulia ionantha 'Englert's Diana' (opposite top)
Anthurium scherzerianum (opposite bottom)

the block and allowed to remain for five minutes. When watering, never wet the crown.

Spring- and Summer-flowering
Anthurium scherzerianum, which has the popular name of the Flamingo Plant, because of its brilliant and spectacular scarlet spathes or leaf-like bracts and tail-like orange-red spadix, which is a flower with a fleshy stem. The brilliance of vermilion and bright scarlet makes it a striking highlight in decor. It is hard to grow under ordinary room conditions, because of its almost insatiable demand for constantly moist and warm air. It must have good light, be plunged in wet peat, be watered and syringed freely in summer and kept dryish in winter at not lower than 55°–60°F. (13°–15·5°C.).

Spring- to Autumn-flowering
Spathiphyllum wallisii (Peace Lily), shown in this picture, is an evergreen, with attractive bright, shining green, lance-shaped, pointed leaves. They are 6 to 10 inches long. Its arresting feature is the delicate, white flower (spadix), which is carried on a thin stalk, rising up through the leaves and is surrounded by a white or green spathe, like the arum lily. Not easy to grow under ordinary room conditions, because of its great need for moist air, it should be put in a semi-shady spot in which the humidity is maintained by spraying and plunging its pot in moist peat.

Summer- to Autumn-flowering
Aphelandra squarrosa 'Louisae' is a good form of the Zebra Plant. This somewhat difficult-to-grow plant, despite this disadvantage, is quite a popular one. Possibly this is because it has two attractions; first as a foliage plant with the most striking 9-inch long, dark green, shiny, lance-shaped leaves, carried in pairs, with their veins highlighted with ivory; and

second as a flowering house plant with spectacular yellow flower bracts, each segment of which produces an ivory, tubular-shaped flower. It likes a warm, light spot and to be watered, syringed and fed well in summer, with less in winter.

Summer-flowering
Campanula isophylla is a charming, prostrate plant, which is either white or lilac-blue. There is another beautiful form, *Campanula isophylla* 'Mayi', which has variegated foliage and delightful China-blue flowers. *Campanula isophylla* is really lovely when allowed to hang over the side of a container. Unlike the majority of the members of its large family, it is not hardy and better grown indoors, where it should be given a cool, airy, draught-free, well-lit place. It needs good watering and feeding in summer, reducing it in the winter, when it should be kept at a temperature of 45°–50°F. (7°–10°C.).

Citrus mitis, the Calamondin Orange Tree, is another very beautiful, dual-purpose plant, which has the most lovely, dainty, white, fragrant flowers and produces very delightful small oranges in the autumn. To ensure a crop it is necessary to pollinate by transferring the pollen with a camel-hair brush. The fruits are edible and rather sour, but they can be used in mixing drinks and, if plentiful, to make marmalade. It does well in a cool, airy, bright window, never exposed to frost. It needs frequent watering during the spring and summer. The leaves should be syringed when it is hot.

Hibiscus rosa-sinensis, Chinese rose, is an attractive, small shrub with large, exotic, trumpet-shaped flowers, which fade in a day or so, to be succeeded by their equally colourful

Spathiphyllum wallisii (left)
Aphelandra squarrosa (right)
Campanula isophylla (opposite)
Citrus mitis (overleaf)

counterpart. White, pink and red varieties are obtainable. There is also *Hibiscus rosa-sinensis* 'Cooperi', which is variegated with rather less numerous red flowers. It thrives in very light surroundings and needs full sun to flower. Bud production is stimulated by pruning in early spring. When the buds form, the plant must not be moved. Water and syringe well, reducing it in winter, when the temperature must not be less than 55°F. (13°C.).

Aechmea fasciata (top)
Hibiscus rosa-sinensis (bottom)

Bromeliads

Aechmea fasciata, which makes the most beautiful and fascinating house plant, is called by some the Fascination Plant. Another common name is the Urn Plant, because the leaves form a funnel-shaped rosette with a central vase. The greyish-green, strap-like leaves are most striking with their whitish, horizontal bands and the flowering spike, which rises through the funnel, consisting of tiny, inconspicuous flowers and prominent pinkish bracts, remains in colour for six months. Cultivation is fairly easy; it should not be kept too wet, even in summer, but the central 'vase' should always have some water in. It likes a well-lit spot.

Billbergia nutans is another fascinating member of the Pineapple family. It has spiny, narrow, rush-like leaves, which form a rosette at the base from which arise long flowering stalks carrying at their ends nodding, colourful, exotic-looking blooms, that are composed of large conspicuous rosy bracts and small yellowish green flowers. Easily cultivated, it tolerates cool conditions, dry air and gas fumes in the atmosphere.

Nevertheless flowering is encouraged by good light and warmth and it should be fed, but not over-watered, during summer. All the dead flowers should be removed with tweezers, leaving the bracts.

Vriesia splendens is another beautiful, spectacular bromeliad and is known as Painted Feathers. Its large strap-like leaves, that are banded brown and soft green in colour and dark reddish brown on the reverse, form a funnel-shaped rosette with a central vase, which is kept filled with water.

From this base there emerges a flower spike, which bears at its top a bright scarlet, spear-shaped bract, which might be at least 2 feet long. Although it tolerates a dark corner, it prefers to stand in good light. It should have a winter temperature of not less than 55°F. (13°C.).

Billbergia nutans (below)
Vriesia splendens (opposite)

Flowering Pot Plants

Easy-to-Grow Plants

Winter Flowering

Solanum capsicastrum is variously known as the Winter, Jerusalem or Christmas Cherry. Although the plant is much cherished for its charming display of orange or red berries during winter, it does also have pretty white flowers. The fruits will remain for months, if the plant is kept free from gas and draughts in a moist atmosphere and in a light place. Water and spray regularly, with occasional feeding, until the berries fall. It is usual to buy fresh plants every year, but pruned back hard and put in the garden during the summer months, *Solanum capsicastrum* will usually survive.

Camellia japonica 'Kimberley'. A camellia, with its dark green, shiny leaves makes a pleasing indoor plant with its brilliantly coloured, waxen blooms enlivening the dark, winter days. It is a good idea to buy a potted plant in flower after Christmas and have it indoors until the blooms fade; afterwards keeping it in a cool place in the house until the frosts

Solanum capsicastrum (top)
Camellia japonica 'Kimberley' (bottom)
Cinerarias (opposite top)
Primula obconica (opposite below)

have gone and then planting it outside. A camellia does well on the sill of a window facing north, providing there are no draughts, because the latter, together with dryness and cold, cause bud dropping. Keep it moist.

Winter- and Spring-flowering
Cineraria. The picture (page 51) shows a delightful group of these much appreciated pot plants, which are botanically named *Senecio cruentus*. Their beautiful, large, fresh, pale green leaves and their many daisy-like flowers, forming multi-coloured cushions, give almost phenomenal brilliance to any drawing room during the greater part of winter and spring. Plants are easily purchased and are by no means demanding in their needs. Good light, but not direct sunlight, cool, draught-free conditions, with frequent watering and feeding occasionally in spring and summer are the main factors in success. Spraying with water eliminates greenfly, which are partial to them.

Primula obconica. It is sad to have to commence dealing with this charming plant by issuing a danger warning that its leaves are able to cause a skin rash. So anybody with a sensitive skin should never handle it without wearing rubber gloves. Despite this it is one of the most common indoor primulas grown, possibly because of its large-sized flowers. Also with large, attractive, blooms is *Primula sinensis*. Its flowers are pink, lilac and white; it has velvet leaves. Both *P. obconica* and *P. sinensis* can be kept from one season to another.

Another very attractive plant is *Primula malacoides* (not illustrated), which has rather smaller flowers, more usually lilac in colour, but there are pink, rose and white varieties as well.

Primula kewensis (top)
Calceolaria (bottom)
Fuchsia (opposite)

Primula × kewensis is a valuable winter-flowering plant with large and scented, golden-yellow blooms. Like all primulas, it has a long flowering period. Primulas like to be put in a place that is well-lit, free from draughts, fairly cool and out of direct sun. To ensure a succession of brilliantly coloured blooms, dead flowers should be removed regularly and they should be watered and fed continuously during the flowering season.

Pelargonium hortorum (below)
Pelargonium domestium (opposite)
Achimenes (overleaf)

Spring- and Summer-flowering
Calceolaria is also known as the Slipper Flower. They are very useful plants that range in height from 9 inches to 3 feet. Although they are not everybody's favourite, it cannot be denied that they are most colourful and, with their pouch-like and spotted blooms, are almost sensational, particularly the giant ones. It is usual to buy them potted and discard them after flowering. They thrive well, if stood out of sun on the sill of a well-lit window, where the conditions are cool and airy. Generous watering and occasional feeding during spring and summer are appreciated.

The very beautiful *Fuchsia* illustrated on page 53 is one of many varieties of this exceptionally lovely and graceful plant. With its two-part flowers drooping so charmingly from their flowering stalks, it cannot be a surprise to anybody to learn that they are so aptly nicknamed Lady's Eardrops. It is possible to obtain both trailing and upright plants. The former are most effective when grown in a hanging basket. They like a cool place and to be well watered, fed and sprayed regularly during the growing season. They should not be moved when in bud. The dead flowers should be removed.

Geraniums have been for many generations a great favourite among indoor plants. They are known as *Pelargonium* × *hortorum* and are members of the vast geranium family and derived largely from *P. zonale*. There are many varieties with a wide range of shades, including some miniatures, that do not exceed 3 inches in height. The more vigorous cultivars can be trained on trellis to form colourful room dividers. The ivy geraniums (*P. peltatum*) are very excellent for hanging baskets, but they are not so easy to grow as the bush. Success with geraniums comes with keeping them on a sunny window-sill, watering and feeding them freely in summer and regularly deadheading.

The flower shown in the picture on page 55 is typical of one of the most beautiful of all flowering indoor plants, *P.* × *domestium*, the Regal pelargonium, derived from various species. The many varieties are all showy and free-flowering plants, producing the most gorgeous close-packed clusters of large and beautifully marked flowers in many shades of pink, cerise, red and maroon varying in intensity to almost black, as well as white. The length of their flowering season is shorter than the Zonal pelargoniums. Cultivation is much the same as for the latter. Although renewing them annually is better, kept cool and fairly dry, they will over-winter.

Summer-flowering
Achimenes is a very beautiful plant that is not difficult to grow. It has two popular names; the first is Cupid's Bower and the second is the Hot-water Plant. There are a number of hybrids with funnel-shaped flowers of various colours. *Achimenes* needs a warm, well-lit place. Small tubers can be bought and planted $\frac{1}{2}$ inch deep in potting compost in early spring. As the plants grow they need staking. It should be watered with tepid water without wetting the leaves. After flowering, it is allowed to dry out, cut down and the tubers are removed and saved for next spring.

Summer- and Autumn-flowering
The tuberous begonias are the most popular type for growing in pots for flowers in summer and autumn. Undoubtedly this is because they are so spectacular with, in some cases, huge

Dwarf *Chrysanthemum* (below)
Begonia 'Sugar Candy' (opposite)

flowers. There are both single and double varieties, and there are some with frilled petals. Their colours are some of the most brilliant, as well as some of the most delicate, to be found among any flowers. They include various shades of yellow, orange, red and pink, and some varieties are white. The illustration shows the *Begonia* 'Sugar Candy'. The tubers can be kept from year to year.

All-the-Year-Round Flowering
The picture shows a dwarf chrysanthemum. Chrysanthemums do not naturally bloom throughout the year, but because of modern light controls, it is possible to have a plant in flower always available. Furthermore, although naturally dwarf plants exist, by using dwarfing compounds nurserymen can offer pot versions of many of the taller varieties. The potted chrysanthemums remain in flower for many weeks, after which they are usually discarded. Such plants revert to the taller variety, if planted in the garden. Chrysanthemums need air, coolness, good light and regular watering. It is advantageous to spray the leaves occasionally.

Harder-to-Grow Plants

Winter-flowering
Possibly one of the more attractive and colourful flowering plants is the popular *Cyclamen persicum*, which is so aptly called the Persian Violet. Not only do its flowers, in a wide range of shades of pink, crimson, cerise and salmon-scarlet, make it desirable, but so do its lovely marbled, heart-shaped leaves. The illustration shows *Cyclamen persicum* 'Rose Van Aalsmeer'. Cyclamen like a light position out of sunlight, where it is humid, draught-free and fairly cool. They should be watered from below, avoiding splashing the fleshy crown as it might rot. Regular feeding and deadheading during flowering should be done.

The Cape Heaths are pretty members of the genus *Erica*, several hundred species of which are found in the kinder climate of South Africa. Unfortunately they are not hardy enough to grow outdoors in temperate areas, but there are several that are offered as indoor plants. They readily drop their leaves under normal room conditions. The best way to handle them is to give them a light, cool situation, where there is no direct sunlight, to maintain a moist atmosphere around them by surrounding them with moist peat and to keep their soil always damp.

Cyclamen persicum 'Rose Van Aalsmeer' (top)
Erica 'Cape Heaths' (bottom)
Euphorbia pulcherrima (opposite)

Poinsettia, Euphorbia pulcherrima, now becoming very popular in Britain, has long been a traditional Christmas flower in the United States. What appear to be glorious red, or sometimes pink, flowers are really bracts or flower leaves surrounding the rather insignificant, bright yellow flowers. The old varieties could be rather straggly and difficult, but worthwhile, pot plants with a tendency to leaf fall, if the conditions were not suitable. The modern varieties have overcome these problems to some degree and are generally more compact growing. If it is possible they should be given a humid atmosphere, be sprayed periodically and be watered cautiously, never waterlogged. They also need a good light and to be kept fairly warm in the absence of draughts and gas fumes.

Azaleas are very popular shrubs with small evergreen leaves and the varieties and hybrids of *Rhododendron indicum* and *R. simsii* form the bulk of those grown as house plants (azalea is a section of the rhododendron family). Its red, pink or white flowers engulf nearly all the plant for several months during winter. It is not always found to be easy to grow, because it must have moist air, no draughts and a fairly warm, steady temperature. Success can be achieved by keeping it in a well-lit, airy spot away from direct sunlight, watering freely and preferably with rainwater so the soil is always damp. Plunged in the shade outdoors during the summer and brought indoors in autumn, it will live from year to year.

Azalea (top)
Gloxinea 'Emperor Frederick' (bottom)
Coleus 'Rainbow Strain' (opposite)

Summer-flowering

The illustration left is one of *Gloxinia* (*Sinningia speciosa*) 'Emperor Frederick', which is representative of a large range of varieties, which all have brilliantly coloured, sometimes spotted, large, handsome, bell-shaped flowers. Being more suitable to greenhouses, gloxinias are rather on the difficult side to grow in most rooms, but they are so lovely that it is well worth the effort to succeed. The ingredients of success are to stand them in a light, fairly warm position, out of direct sunlight, keeping the atmosphere humid. When watering (with tepid water) avoid wetting the leaves and flowers.

Gloxinias like regular feeding during flowering time.

It is perhaps an anomaly to ally coleus to the flowering pot plants. Apart from the convenience, there is some justification for doing so, because the intensity and variation of the colour of its leaves rival that of the colours of many flowering plants. In the illustration is a grouping of *Coleus* 'Rainbow Strain'. Coleus does have flowers, but they are very uninteresting and should be picked off to divert the energy to the leaves. It needs plenty of light and water, to be free from draughts, a moist atmosphere, particularly in winter, and winter temperatures of not below 55°F. (13°C.).

Palms

Neanthe bella is regarded as the best palm for growing in the house. It is small, reaching eventually 4 feet high, and easy to grow. The long pinnate and bright green leaves, hang gracefully making it attractive as a single specimen; it is excellent as the pinnacle in an arrangement and it adds charm to a bottle garden. It should be given a light position out of direct sunlight, watered freely in summer and sparingly in winter. It much appreciates having its leaves sponged or sprayed occasionally as it particularly dislikes a hot and dry atmosphere in which the leaves will turn brown.

Howea forsteriana, the Kentia Palm, the Flat or Thatch Leaf Palm, is another somewhat smaller type of palm. For some years it will make a good plant for house cultivation, although it will ultimately grow 6 feet high and might then be an embarrassment. It is regarded by some as the best of the palms as a house plant. A close relative, *Howea belmoreana,* the Curly Palm, is also suitable for this purpose and is a rather slower grower, and it is more elegant. Both have graceful pendulous leaves. Their needs are much the same as those of *Neanthe bella*.

Neanthe bella (top)
Howea forsteriana (bottom)

Ferns

other feature in the decor where it is effective. It has two kinds of leaves—firstly upstanding green ones like the antlers of a stag and secondly pale green ones, that become brown paper-like, which clasp tightly to whatever object the fern is attached.

Easy-to-Grow Plants

Nephrolepsis exalta, which is among the most beautiful of ferns, has a multiplicity of popular names—Boston Fern, Curly Fern, Crested Ladder Fern, Sword Fern, Whitman Fern. The fronds are 2 feet long or even more, with leaflets (pinnae) up to 3 inches long and $\frac{1}{2}$ inch wide. It is stately and tall, which qualities are especially exemplified, as shown in the illustration, when grown on its own in a pot. Yet at the same time there is a smoothness about the manner in which its large fronds gracefully droop, that makes it, either singly or with others, superb for growing in hanging baskets.

Platycerium alcicorne, the Stag's-horn Fern, is a unique plant, that comes from Australia. Because of its habit of growth it can be effectively grown either in a pot or more naturally on a pad of moss that is kept constantly moist, tied to a piece of bark, which can be attached to a wall or to any

Platycerium alcicorne (top)
Nephrolepsis exalta (bottom)

Harder-to-Grow Plants

Maidenhair Fern, *Adiantium capillus veneris*, is a comparatively easy pot plant to grow, but it is not the easiest of the house ferns to cultivate. This is because it must have moist, pure air all the time. It also likes to live in partial shade. It also requires to be watered frequently, preferably with rainwater, so that the soil is always moist. These are the conditions that it enjoys in its natural surroundings. It should be free from draughts, smoke and gas fumes. The ideal place for it is a bottle garden. If possible, a spell in a warm, moist greenhouse does a potted plant good.

Asplenium nidus, which is popularly known as the Bird's Nest Fern, is not the easiest fern to grow in large towns, particularly because like all members of its family it hates smoke, fumes and dust. It is a very striking plant, with its very bright green leaves, with a deeply impressed central vein and slightly wavy margins, that unlike many ferns, are not divided. They eventually grow 2 to 4 feet long and 3 to 8 inches wide and emerge from the base to form what is like a giant shuttlecock. *Asplenium nidus* likes a shady, warm, moist place with its soil kept damp continuously.

Adiantium capillus veneris (below)
Asplenium nidis (opposite)

Bulbs

Hyacinth 'Jan Bos' (top)
Daffodils (bottom)
Crocus vernus (opposite left)
Amaryllis hippeastrum (opposite bottom)
Vallota speciosa (opposite right)

Annual Plants

Hyacinth 'Jan Bos'. For flowers at Christmas, specially prepared hyacinth bulbs must be bought and planted four months earlier. When they are taken from the dark, any unwanted side shoots should be cut off. When preparing bowls for indoors the question that many people ask is "at what depth beneath surface of the fibre should the bulbs be planted?"

Here are some general rules:

Hyacinths and daffodils with their noses just visible.
Tulips just covered.
Small bulbs: tips $\frac{1}{4}$ to $\frac{1}{2}$ inch below.

Specially cultivated narcissi bulbs can be bought which, if they are planted in early autumn and the instructions accompanying them are followed, will be in bloom on Christmas Day. Spring-flowering crocuses are delightful, colourful flowers to have also indoors at this festive time.

A general procedure for growing indoors is given below:

Pack into the bowl moist fibre to such a height that it will support bulbs placed on it at the correct planting level.
Stand the bulbs on this surface and pack fibre around them to the right height.
Place the bowl in a dark, cool place for 8–10 weeks (10–12 for daffodils) or until the flower buds of crocuses and other small bulbs show colour. This place might be buried in a box of sand in the garden, a

cupboard or cellar or an upturned box or tent of black polythene in the corner of a room.
After this time, when the shoots are probably 2–3 inches long, bring the bowl out into the light to a cool, shady place. When the growth greens up in about 7 days, transfer it to a warmer, lighter spot.

Permanent Bulbs

Amaryllis (Hippeastrum) has spectacular flowers and is easy to grow in the house. Plant the bulb in potting compost in mid-October so that it is halfway out of the soil. Give it bottom warmth by placing it on a warm shelf, say, over a radiator. When buds form, transfer to a sunny window-sill, watering sparingly at first and then freely, **always from the top.** To keep for the next season, put it in a cool place after flowering, watering until growth stops and then almost cease. Next spring, top-dress with fresh soil and increase watering steadily.

Vallota speciosa (Vallota purpurea) is a beautiful permanent bulb plant, that is popularly known as the Scarborough Lily. It has heads of flowers, that are scarlet and sometimes other tones of red, or white in late summer. Further loveliness lies in the fact that its foliage is evergreen. Easy to grow, it thrives in two parts sandy loam and one part leaf-mould which should be kept just damp during autumn and winter, with increased watering and feeding in spring and summer. It likes a sunny window. It should remain in the same pot for three or four years.

Cacti and Succulents

member that is popular, is *M. bocasana*, which has fine, grey-white spines and thick hairs, among which, almost hidden from sight, are its yellowish flowers with a reddish stripe on the outer petals, that are produced profusely.

It is the practice to separate 'Cacti' and 'Succulents' and this convention has been followed in this book. Strictly succulents are plants that because of drought conditions, that persist in their habitat, have developed thick, fleshy tissues within their stems and leaves so that water loss by evaporation is reduced and they can store water. Cacti, which have these characteristics, are therefore really succulents. The cacti and succulents described here are all easy to grow.

Cacti

The cacti in the illustration below is *Mammillaria wildii*, which is one of a large species that can be recommended to beginners because they resist adversity, even to the extent of withstanding erroneous treatment and neglect. *M. wildii* is among the hardiest of the species. It has soft flesh, yellow, hooked spines and whitish flowers in a ring at the top. Another

Chamaecereus silvestrii (top)
Mammillaria wildii (bottom)
Echinocereus blanckii (opposite top)
Echinopsis eyriesii (opposite bottom)

Chamaecereus silvestrii is commonly known as the Peanut Cactus. It is composed of bunches of thick, soft, jointed stems dotted with spines. These produce small sections or branch-lets, that are easily removed or drop off naturally, which resemble peanuts and hence its popular name. Numerous beautiful, erect, bell-shaped, vermilion blooms, with golden anthers poised on reddish filaments adorn this cactus in early spring, emerging from its branches. It is easily grown and should be in any collection. During its growing season it needs light, warmth and water, but in winter, being mountainous in origin, it requires light, dry, cold surroundings.

Echinopsis eyriesii is another popular cactus that flourishes under almost any conditions. As seen in the picture, the growth is spherical in shape. This is the juvenile form of the cactus, which can reach a diameter of about 8 inches. After this it becomes adult and columnar growing some 3 feet high. Very attractive, white flowers emerge from near the top of these globes, which have shining, dark green skin. *Echinopsis eyriesii* requires a heavier rich soil with slight shade and adequate watering while growing, and occasional watering, light and a temperature not below 50°F. (10°C.) in winter. It hails from South America.

Echinocereus blanckii is probably one of the most colourful of all desert cacti. It should be mentioned that there are two types of cactus that are grown indoors; the desert or terrestrial cacti and the epiphytic cacti. The former, as the name suggests, are found growing in the hot, arid conditions of the deserts of such places as Mexico. When cultivated they require these natural conditions to be simulated. The epiphytic cacti grow in their natural surroundings on trees and rocks. They

Astrophytum myriostigma (top)
Parodia microsperma (bottom)
Opuntia microdasys (opposite)

live on decaying vegetable debris blown by the winds and washed to their roots. Thus they are not parasites.

It requires no imagination to see how *Astrophytum myriostigma* got its nickname of Bishop's Mitre. It is an easy-to-grow cactus and is a great favourite. Although when young it is globular, with age it becomes columnar and reaches a height of some 24 inches. The green skin is covered thickly with small, grey-white felted spots. From its crown arise, often several at a time, attractive, large, pale yellow flowers, which are $1\frac{1}{2}$ to $2\frac{1}{2}$ inches in diameter. It flourishes with adequate sunlight and watering, when growing. In winter it needs dry, light conditions at about 50°F. (10°C.).

Parodia microsperma is a member of a large genus of cacti, many of which are easy to cultivate. It was an early *Parodia* to be discovered and was found at the end of the nineteenth century in the mountains of Argentina. In common with some other members of its genus, its body is flattened spherical, becoming slightly columnar as it ages. It is bright green in colour and covered with many fairly long spines. The most attractive feature is its orange-yellow flowers that emerge easily and freely near its crown in spring, remaining in flower for quite a long time.

Shown on page 73 is the cactus, *Opuntia microdasys,* which is the much jointed plant on the right, planted in the company of Haworthias, which are succulents. Nobody looking at this cactus can have any illusions regarding how it got its two nicknames Prickly Pear and Bunny's Ears. Probably it is one of the most fascinating of cacti to grow indoors with its shrublike formation, composed of flattened oval pads, that are emerald green in colour. The very small, yellowish-brown, barbed bristles make it look as if it is clothed in wool. It is extremely tolerant, and can be cultivated with no difficulty. Also shown in the illustration is a typical succulent of the genus *Haworthia*.

Rebutia marsoneri is an easily grown cactus, which should be in every beginner's collection. It is a small plant with a flattened spherical body, which eventually grows about $2\frac{1}{2}$ inches high and $3\frac{1}{2}$ inches in diameter. Pale green in colour, ultimately becoming grey at the base, it is covered with spines that vary in colour from white to deep yellow. It has intensely red buds, that break into beautiful golden-yellow flowers. The discovery of *Rebutia marsoneri* in 1935 was a sensation in the cactus-world, because all the hitherto-known rebutias had flowers of varying red shades.

Aporocactus flagelliformis, has long, glossy, green stems, later becoming grey, resembling rat's tails. Hence its popular name is the Rat's Tail Cactus. It is seen in the illustration below on the right with some succulents. The spines are reddish, later becoming brown. It has very lovely, colourful, profuse flowers, that are 3 inches long, emerging from the stems. There are a number of hybrids that produce flowers in abundance that are in a range of colours. A beautiful one of these is *Aporocactus flagelliformis* 'Vulkan', which has scarlet flowers. An epiphytic plant, it requires rich soil and adequate watering.

Epiphyllum ackermannii is a very delightful epiphytic cactus, that has the very appropriate and descriptive popular name, the Orchid Cactus. It has flattened, dark stems with a few spines, from which emerge its gorgeous flowers. Even more popular today are its numerous hybrids, that bloom in the summer. Notable among these are 'Cooperi', with large white,

Rebutia marsoneri (top)
Aporocactus flagelliformis (bottom)
Epiphyllum ackermannii (opposite)

scented flowers, 'London Glory', with its orange-red and magenta flowers and the strongly fragrant 'London Surprise' which has large, orange blooms. Like other epiphytes they need to have peat and a little well-rotted manure incorporated in their soil to retain the moisture.

Zygocactus truncatus, the Christmas Cactus, is one of the best known and appreciated of the epiphytic cacti. It derives its nickname from the fact that it usually blooms in November and is in flower on Christmas Day. It is often at its best at Christmas-time when its cerise-purple flowers with their many petals, like tassels, spring from the ends of its pendulous, jointed, greyish green stems. Incidentally this means that it is growing in winter and unlike some other cacti it needs to be watered during that season. There are orange and white varieties, but they are rarer.

Rhipsalidopsis gaertneri, once known as *Schlumbergera*

gaertneri, is still sold under that name. It is sometimes called the Easter Cactus, because it blooms from Easter onwards, although this name is also given to a relative, *Rhipsalidopsis rosea.* It is an epiphytic cactus and requires the conditions appropriate to these plants. It has the pendulous, spreading habit of *Zygocactus truncatus* and its colourful flowers are produced, sometimes in groups, from the top joint of its stems. It can be grown in a pot and is quite happy in a hanging basket or on sphagnum moss, attached to a piece of bark.

Zygocactus truncatus (opposite)
Rhipsalidopsis gaertneri (below)

Succulents

Kalanchoe blossfeldiana is a member of a genus of plants with a very large number of species, but it is one of two, that are striking for their flowers and is the best known. It has panicles of charming, red flowers and a delightful shrubby form. A valuable succulent because it blooms so brilliantly in the winter, when, of course, it must be kept watered. There are several varieties offered by seedsmen—they are not difficult to raise from seed, if heat is available. These include 'Morning Sun', which has star-shaped old gold blooms and dwarf scarlet 'Vulcan'.

Stapelia variegata, as will be seen in the illustration, is difficult to describe adequately. To some it might be bizarre, perhaps objectionable, while to others it might be a fantasy recalling for them some picture in a fairy-tale book that still lingers in their mind. This curious and quite beautiful, plant with its smooth, 6-inch long, branching, light green, mottled leaves, bearing teeth-like prominencies and its five-petalled, star-like, variably coloured flowers with brown and yellow speckles and stripes scattered over them, might well fit into a modern decor. It flowers continuously during summer into late autumn.

Euphorbia splendens is a very attractive, succulent member of the same plant family as the poinsettia. It is characterised by its long, sharp thorns, which can be most damaging to the hands, if it is handled carelessly. These give the plant its rather frightening common name of the Crown of Thorns. With its

bright, scarlet bracts, produced in pairs, it makes a decorative pot plant that grows ultimately to a height of 3 feet. It gives little trouble, being seldom attacked by pests or diseases. It likes a winter temperature of about 45°F. (7°C.). During this period it requires little watering.

Euphorbia splendens (below)

Orchids

Cymbidium 'Ramley'. Many fight shy of growing orchids, primarily in the belief that they are far beyond their capabilities and because at least some may feel that they are only for the very rich, who can afford elaborate hot-houses and specialist gardeners to attend their inmates. For this reason they are seldom dealt with in books on indoor plants. Not all of them, however, need hot-house care; some can grow in a normal room. Among these are the *cymbidiums,* one of which is illustrated opposite, the coelogynes and the cypripedium group. They are all showy plants.

This delightful orchid, *Pleione pricei,* is representative of another group that can be grown in the house. These orchids were discovered, often on the snowline, in the Himalayas and are quite hardy and easy to grow. During the winter they need no attention except ensuring that they are not exposed to frost. During the summer months, pleiones should be watered copiously, never being allowed to dry out. An occasional liquid feed is beneficial. They should be repotted annually either before or just after flowering, in a rich mixture of peat or loam, containing some dried farmyard manure and sand.

Cymbidium 'Ramley' (opposite)
Pleione pricei (below)

Bonsai

This picture shows a very charming Bonsai *Pyracantha*, which has been trained to this intriguing shape. Such manipulation is an integral part of the bonsai art, at which the Japanese are so very skilled. It makes it possible to give a plant an appearance of old age or oddity. This is done by mechanical means, such as winding wire around branches and trunks to enable them to be bent to shape and desired direction, weighing branches down with weights and attaching wires to the trunks and limbs and tying them to pegs driven into the soil to give them a distorted look.

Bonsai—*Picea pungens* 'Glauca' and Chestnut or Buckeye (*Aesculus*). Each is a typical artificially dwarfed tree or 'bonsai'. The bonsai art is one that has been in being in Japan and China for centuries, spreading, first to the U.S., and later to the U.K. Bonsai are charming and fascinating plants that are assets in interior decoration. For this purpose excellent specimens can be bought, but old ones are costly. Anybody can, however, dwarf trees by gathering their seeds and seedlings from the garden and taking cuttings, and planting them in a suitable potting compost. After they have become well-established, the dwarfing process can begin. The procedure is:

Pyracantha (top)
Picea pungens (bottom)
Chestnut (opposite)

Transplant the plants into individual cream cartons with small holes punched in their sides and bottom with a knitting needle, using a weak potting compost recommended by your local plantsman.
Prune for two years any roots that appear through the apertures.
During the second year, shape the plant by pinching out growing tips to encourage bushiness, shortening shoots and removing unwanted ones to make the outline of the dwarf conform to that of its giant counterpart.
At the beginning of the third year, after root pruning, plant the bonsai in poor soil (2 parts of the potting compost and 1 part coarse sand).

Bottle Gardens

An attractive way of growing certain house plants, especially those needing continuous humidity and warmth, is in a glass bottle. It is often a matter of conjecture as to how such plants are planted. Initially tools must be improvised.

A trowel: composed of a shortened, old spoon fixed to a 2 feet long bamboo cane.
A fork-cum-rake: consisting of an old table fork similarly treated.
A rammer: made of a cotton reel with a 2 feet long

bamboo cane, fixed with adhesive, in its hole.
A pair of tongs: a pair of kitchen tongs cut down and fitted with two 2 feet long bamboo canes.

The planting procedure is:

Wash the container out with water and drain it.
Place a layer of stones on the bottom of the bottle.
Put a weak grade potting compost on top of it.
Make a hole in the compost with the trowel for each plant, drop it in and manoeuvre it into position with the tongs.
Cover its roots with soil and firm it round with the rammer.
After planting, close the vessel until the condensation clears. Do not water for 2 months and then very sparingly at long intervals, which may even be a year.

Plants in a carboy (below)
Plants in a flask (opposite)

Plant Arrangements

This ambitious display shows a very beautiful indoor roof garden of a luxury flat. It is comparable with the winter gardens of some very wealthy nineteenth-century households, some of whom had commissioned plant hunters to bring plants from overseas to adorn their expansive conservatories. Many of these were found in tropical forests and needed humidity and heat, which was provided by piped hot water, heated by a coke stove. Hence these plants are known as 'stove plants'. A proportion of the plants growing in this roof garden, which are quite popular house plants today, are the stove plants of former times.

The lovely illustration below is a great contrast to the flamboyant display shown in the picture opposite. Here are two, or perhaps three, very colourful *Saintpaulias* in a delightfully designed china basket. It is a display that might make a very significant mark on the decor of any room; for example as a dining table centre. As is known, *Saintpaulias* are difficult to grow. Among other things they need humid conditions. It would be better therefore to meet this requirement by planting in individual pots and plunging them into moist peat filled in the basket, which should be first lined with polythene.

Probably one of the most popular ways of enjoying indoor plants is in arrangements or dish gardens. Sometimes they are composed entirely of house plants, which is, of course, a permanent display, but often seasonal flowering pot plants are included as is the case with the one shown in the picture opposite. In this case, a cyclamen is giving a high proportion of colour. If this is done, it is probably better to keep the pot plant in a small pot to enable it to be replaced by another one, just about to bloom, when its flowering season is ended.

Above is shown another attractive dish garden which is made up of house plants, which include *Aralia elegantissima*, *Tradescantia* 'Silver Queen', *Begonia rex*, *Codiaeum*, *Philodendron scandens*, *Aglaonema* 'Silver Queen' and *Hedera helix* 'Heisse'. Flower arrangers will recognise the importance of following certain well-established principles, when making an arrangement. Perhaps one of the major ones is to have a pinnacle as a centre, around which to arrange the other plants of varying heights. In this one, the *Philodendron scandens* will soon outstrip its neighbours and form the high point. Sometimes water tubes are incorporated in foliage arrangements to hold cut flowers to give seasonal colour.

This rather appealing trough, made of cane, is one of numerous containers used for displaying house plants. They range from the simple clay pots—sometimes simplicity is valuable, because it does not detract from the beauty of the plant—to elaborate thermostatically heated and continuously lit glass display cases. This trough makes provision for some larger plants, such as *Ficus elastica* 'Decora', *F. benjamina* and *Philodendron* at the top and for climbers like the ivies (*Hedera*) below, that not only climb up their supports, but trespass and picturesquely clamber up the legs of the stand. Plants can be easily removed for attention.

The arrangement in the picture below depicts how effective house plants can be when arranged in a wicker basket. Among them can be recognised *Cyclamen persicum*, the succulent *Kalanchoe blossfeldiana*, *Peperomia*, *Calathea*, *Hedera*, with *Grevillea robusta*, giving the arrangement its pinnacle. The plants are very well arranged and balanced, showing just sufficient of the basket and handle to form an appealing foil to the mainly dark green tones of the growing subjects. When selecting plants for a group in a container, it is most important that those picked out are willing to live side by side under the same conditions.

Very effective live screens can be created using climbing house plants, both foliage and flowering. Such screens can, of course, be made permanent or movable. In this illustration climbers are seen climbing over a structure, which is situated in the window of a room. The plants used are open ones and are sufficient to obscure the view of the windows opposite, which are fairly close, yet do not interfere seriously with the light passing through. Such screens, using climbing house plants, can be effectively stood on the ground to make room dividers in houses or in offices which are open plan design.

There are many different types of vessel that can be used for house plants. Some of them are shown in this picture, which includes a lead (or perhaps, a glass fibre simulation) tub, terracotta troughs and a simple earthenware vase, which all admirably meet the purpose. Almost any container or holder can be adapted to give the utmost satisfaction in this respect. Often the simplest, such as a garden or basket-work trug, can give rise to the most beautiful effect in a room when filled with gay indoor plants. A search among the junk, with some imagination, might prove fruitful to the enthusiast.

gramineus 'Variegatus', none should be allowed to stand permanently in water.

Two excellent ways of conserving moisture, which is very important when going on holiday, are plunging into moist peat and standing on a wet pebble tray as described under *Humidity*.

Fresh Air

A very important part of the life of an indoor plant is being given a blow in the fresh air. This can be done by opening the windows wide or standing them out in the open on a mild day avoiding draughts. A little warm summer rain often does no harm; it helps to wash the foliage of the large-leaved plants. Opening the windows also helps to clear the air in the house of gas fumes, etc., which are objectionable to house plants.

Cleanliness

A good, regular sponging of the large-leaved plants with tepid water adds much to their appearance and gives them a beautiful shine. It serves to remove dirt from their surface and free their pores so that the plant can breathe in the carbon dioxide that is so essential to them. Smaller leaved plants similarly benefit from regular spraying.

Although there are some quite safe proprietary wax polishes on the market, do not use olive oil as sometimes recommended, because it attracts the dust and the pores soon get clogged.

Feeding

Whatever is used for fertilizing the potting compost for house plants, there are two rules that must be observed.

(1) Always give liquid manure when the soil is moist after watering, otherwise the fertilizers will not be effective.

(2) Plants should be only given fertilizer during the growing season. This means in summer and early autumn for foliage and flowering plants that bloom in the summer and from late autumn to spring for winter-flowering ones. On no account should liquid fertilizer be given to plants while they are resting.

There are several proprietary preparations on the market, of which a few drops can be used when watering.

Repotting

Eventually potted indoor plants slow up in growth despite all the regular feeding that is being carried out. The soil dries out very rapidly and the intervals between waterings become less. In addition roots grow through the drainage hole. All these are indications that they are outgrowing their living room and need to be repotted into a pot of the next size (never more than one size larger unless the plant is very vigorous). As a final test of the necessity for repotting, the plant should be carefully removed from the pot. If it is pot-bound, there will be a matted mass of roots on the outside of the ball and it will be difficult to see any soil at all.

It may not be necessary to repot for about two years after the plant has been purchased or originally potted. It is important not to be in too great a hurry to do this because, as strange as it may seem to the inexperienced, most plants flourish more in a pot apparently too small than in a larger one. In addition flowering plants always flower better in a small pot.

Suitable composts are available from garden suppliers and maybe basically improved soils or one of the proprietary soilless composts which might be more readily available to town-dwellers.

Top-dressing

Some very large house plants are not easy to repot. These can be kept going for quite a long time by removing the top two inches of soil annually in spring and replacing it with fresh compost enriched by extra fertilizer.

Health

Fortunately attack by insects is a fairly rare occurrence but if it takes place, it is vitally important to take immediate action, because the depredation of these creatures is so disfiguring that a plant becomes unpleasant to look at. Some of the under-mentioned pests are also common to cacti.

Greenfly (Asphids)

All gardeners and many others know these sap-sucking insects very well indeed. When they infest a plant their green-coloured bodies engulf the stems, leaves and buds. Because they withdraw the sap from them, the leaves and stems become distorted. Fortunately, indoors they never reach the high level of attack that they do out of doors and frequently regular spraying with water will keep them down. If the attack reaches an epidemic scale, the plants should be sprayed with Malathion or Red Arrow or a systemic insecticide.

Red Spider Mite

These troublesome indoor pests show their presence by the formation of a fine, white webbing underneath the leaves. They do not usually appear when the conditions are humid. If they are troublesome, they are best eliminated by spraying with petroleum white oil emulsion, being sure to do this in a place where the insecticide cannot do any damage to furnishing fabrics.

White Flies

These are white moth-like insects and are sap-suckers. The foliage becomes mottled and the plant is covered with a sticky fluid, honeydew. They should be sprayed with Malathion.

Scale Insects

When these are present, the stems and undersides of the leaves become coated with small, off-white, waxy scales. They are best removed from house plants by being rubbed off with a matchstick, tipped with a ball of cotton wool that has been saturated with methylated spirit.

Mealy Bugs

These unusual, small pests look like minute woodlice, covered in a white, waxy secretion, that gives them the appearance of tiny flecks of cotton wool. They are sap-suckers that are found in the joints of the stalks and on the under surface of the leaves during summer. These are best dealt with by the methylated spirit treatment prescribed for scale insects.

The most common diseases to be contended with are rot and mildew. Wherever possible rot should be dealt with immediately it is detected by cutting away the affected areas and eliminating the most likely causes. Steps should be taken to avoid water falling and remaining on the plant. If damage has been done, often the plant will be restored by keeping it in a moderately warm place and only watering sparingly.

Mildew is a disease with which all gardeners are familiar. It is indicated by stems and leaves becoming coated with white powder. Spraying with Karathane or Benomyl, when the disease first appears, is the best control.

Effect of Heat and Light on Indoor Plants

Already it has been mentioned how modern heating and lighting techniques have substantially assisted in the last twenty years or so the great revival in interest in indoor plants by affording people in ordinary homes the means to control more easily the temperature and light conditions under which their plants are kept. Warmth and light are, of course, essential to the well-being of indoor plants and are inter-related.

In the eighteenth and nineteenth centuries, it was fashionable to provide conservatories for non-hardy exotic plants. These were constructed of glass to admit the maximum amount of sunlight, which was then the only source of light suitable for plants, and continuously kept warm, so that there were no great variations in temperature, as there might have been in the living quarters of the house.

The introduction of central heating in more recent years has made it possible to grow house plants more easily in ordinary rooms. This is because it makes it possible to give them conditions under which there are no great differences in temperature, which indoor plants abhor. Ideally the differential between high and low temperatures should not exceed 7° or 8°F. (4° or 4·5°C.). The worse enemy of indoor plants is the unheated room by day with a roasting from a fire during the evening. The next best thing to central heating is a slow-burning, solid fuel stove that burns all night.

The automatic controls inherent to modern systems of central heating give a ready means of bringing about the conditions most needed by indoor plants. For the majority of them, temperatures 15°–21°C. (59°–70°F.) by day and 7°–15°C. (45°–59°F.) by night, with no great fluctuations, should be aimed at. It should also be remembered that in higher temperatures, plants need more light, which affords another means of control.

It is well known that plants need light, but their requirements vary. There are a few that can manage with relatively little, but the majority must have good light. Most modern houses and commercial buildings have spacious windows allowing sunlight to pass freely and creating therefore ideal conditions for indoor plants. Plants are, however, now so popular that people want to use them more and more as part of their interior decoration and put them in places which need brightening up. It is realised that in situations in a house or office which require to be enlivened and beautified, indoor plants are most useful.

Often these spots are not well-lit and this lack of sunlight is a handicap. Such places include dark corridors, corners remote from windows, disused fireplaces, basement flats, offices, restaurants, attics, hotel foyers and other spaces where natural lighting is restricted. Fortunately, however, it has been found that plants do not need sunlight, but can be satisfied by means of artificial lighting.

To achieve this end, it is best to use fluorescent lighting, because ordinary light bulbs or reflector floods create too much heat, particularly in enclosed areas, when used in the numbers necessary to produce the required illumination. The latter varies from plant to plant and the higher the temperature, the more strength of, and exposure to, light is needed.

It has been found that for the best growth, plants should be given a source of light giving a balance of red and blue rays. This can be obtained by illuminating the area with one 40 watt, 4 foot 'daylight' fluorescent tube (for blue waves) and a similar sized 'warm white' (for red). Effective alternatives are two similar, regular, soft white tubes or special fluorescent bulbs that give ultra-violet rays as well as light.

There are optimum light conditions for indoor plants, but these depend upon a number of factors, including the species concerned. It is difficult to stipulate hard and fast rules regarding such things as intensity of the light source, the period of exposure and the distances the plants should be placed from the fluorescent tubes. This is particularly hard when dealing with groupings of plants. It is necessary to compromise and to vary conditions according to the signals given by the plants. The most important of these is that those that are receiving too much fluorescent light tend to turn yellow and should be moved further away from the source or be exposed for a shorter period daily; if they grow unduly long stalks, they must be given more light by either being moved nearer or given a longer daily dose. Although a rough and ready rule, plants exposed to two 40 watt 4 foot fluorescent tubes for 16 hours daily do best, if no more than one yard from them. For rapid initial growth, the plants should be placed three or four inches away, gradually spacing them further as they grow.

Index